In My Town

by Cara Torrance

OXFORD
UNIVERSITY PRESS
AUSTRALIA & NEW ZEALAND

T0362679

My Town, Your Town

There are many different places in a town. Each place has an important **role** in town life.

A town has schools, sports fields, shops and parks. Many towns have a medical clinic and a vet clinic. There might be a recycling station or a shared garden.

School

People teach and learn in a school. People can also come together to see shows, play sports and hold meetings.

These people are performing in a play.

A school is very important in a town. People can make friends there. They can gain a sense of pride and **belonging**.

Park

There is a lot to do in a park. You can play and meet with friends. You can walk the dog. The local park is a good spot for people to enjoy some fresh air.

Many people enjoy playing sports at a park.

You might meet other people who live in your town at the park, maybe even people you know. Sometimes you can see special **events**, such as a musical show.

Shops

There are many kinds of shops in a town. You might find supermarkets and clothes shops. There may be a garden or sports shop. Having these shops in town makes it easy to get the things you need.

Supermarkets help us shop for the food we need.

Many people work in shops. These jobs are important. They help everyone in the town.

Vet Clinic

You can get help for your pet at a vet clinic. People who take care of animals work there.

vet

You can take your pet to the vet if it is sick or hurt. A vet works to keep the town's pets healthy.

This dog is having a check-up.

Medical Clinic

You can get help at a medical clinic if you are sick or hurt. Nurses and doctors work at medical clinics.

We're here to help you if you are sick.

A medical clinic helps keep the people of a town healthy. It offers help and care to all who need it.

Farmers Market

Farmers and others can sell **goods** at a farmers market. They can sell things they have grown or made.

This bread is for sale at the farmers market.

A farmers market serves the local town. It offers fresh, healthy food and other goods for sale.

Shared Garden

A shared garden is a place where people meet to work together. They plant and grow food to share. They learn about gardening.

You can learn about plants at a shared garden.

A shared garden is good for a town. People without gardens can grow plants and food at a shared garden.

Recycling Station

Rubbish from the town can go to the recycling station to be sorted. Cardboard, paper and glass are separated out. They can then be recycled.

This paper will now be recycled.

A recycling station means that less rubbish goes to **landfill**. This helps us look after our town and the planet.

Electronics, like televisions and computers, can be recycled too.

About Town

Different places in a town help us in different ways. They are all important to a town.

They help meet the needs of the people who live there. They make everyone feel part of the town.

Places and their main uses

Place	Role
School	Teaching and learning
Park	Playing sport and meeting people
Shops	Shopping for things we need
Vet Clinic	Providing pet care
Medical clinic	Providing health care
Farmers market	Shopping for fresh produce
Shared garden	Growing food
Recycling station	Recycling rubbish

Glossary

belonging: feeling as if you are part of something

electronics: items like televisions and computers

events: something that happens, like a music show

goods: things that you pay someone for

landfill: rubbish that is put in the ground

role: the purpose of something

Index